BUILDING THE TRANSCONTINENTAL RAILROAD

Written by **Linda Thompson**

rourkeeducationalmedia.com

Scan for Related Titles
and Teacher Resources

www.rourkeeducationalmedia.com
Courtesy Bancroft Library: page 13; Courtesy California State Railroad Museum Foundation: page 19; Dellenbaugh, Frederick S., Breaking the Wilderness, 1905: pages 26, 30, 34; Courtesy Library of Congress, Prints and Photographs Division: Title page, pages 10, 14, 25, 27, 32, 42; Courtesy Library of Congress, Rare Book and Special Collections Division: pages 8, 16, 41; Courtesy NASA: page 7; Courtesy National Archives and Records Administration: Cover, pages 11, 36; Courtesy National Parks Service: page 36 Courtesy Scotts Bluff National Monument: pages 21, 26, 28-29, 31, 38; Courtesy Union Pacific Railroad: page 15.

Edited by Jill Sherman

Cover design by Nicola Stratford, bdpublishing.com

Interior Layout by Tara Raymo

Library of Congress PCN Data

Thompson, Linda
Building The Transcontinental Railroad / Linda Thompson
ISBN 978-1-62169-839-5 (hard cover)
ISBN 978-1-62169-734-3 (soft cover)
ISBN 978-1-62169-943-9 (e-Book)
Library of Congress Control Number: 2013936388

Rourke Educational Media
Printed in the United States of America,
North Mankato, Minnesota

rourkeeducationalmedia.com
customerservice@rourkeeducationalmedia.com • PO Box 643328 Vero Beach, Florida 32964

TABLE OF CONTENTS

Chapter 1

BUILDING THE TRANSCONTINENTAL RAILROAD

When the 19th century began, the United States had only 17 states and one large territory. The country's western border was the Mississippi River. But by the end of 1803, President Thomas Jefferson had bought the vast and unknown land called Louisiana from France. Stretching from the Mississippi River to the Rocky Mountains, it included 828,000 square miles (2,144,510 square kilometers) of unknown land.

Before the railroad was built, explorers and traders headed west in carts pulled by livestock.

In the 1840s, families began to head west in covered wagons drawn by mules or oxen. The journey by wagon took four months or more. Many people and animals died on this difficult journey. By the 1850s, stagecoaches pulled by fast horses began to carry mail and passengers from the Missouri River to the West Coast in less than three weeks. But nothing could carry heavy loads, such as timber, coal, steel, or livestock better than a train.

RAILROAD FEVER

In 1829, an engineer named Horatio Allen brought one of the new "Iron Horses" from England and tested it on a 3-mile (4.8 kilometer) section of track at a Pennsylvania coal mine. Within a few years, railroad fever had swept the country. By 1840, the East Coast had nearly 3,000 miles (4,800 kilometers) of track, more than in all of Europe. In February 1854, railroads reached the Mississippi River. And 10 years later, there were 33,860 miles (54,200 kilometers) of completed railway in the United States, with 16,000 more miles (25,745 kilometers) under construction.

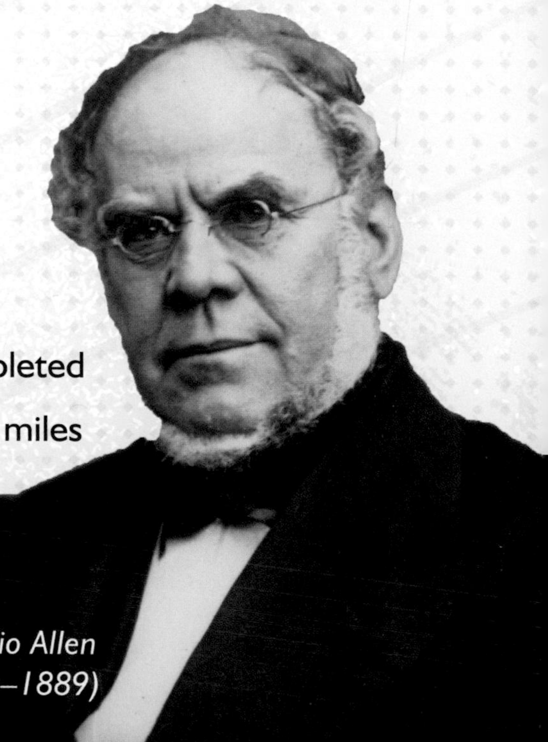

Horatio Allen (1802–1889)

As early as 1830, politicians and others had talked about ways to build a **transcontinental** railroad, linking the Atlantic and Pacific coasts. But many problems had to be solved first. Just getting supplies, including tons of timber and steel, to the point of construction would be very expensive.

Much of the land the tracks would cross had few people aside from **nomadic** groups of Native Americans, who followed the buffalo. They could be expected to strongly resist any railroad across their lands. They knew it could bring thousands of people and the eventual loss of their way of life and their land. It would cost millions of dollars to find good workers to build the railroad, feed them during the 6 to 10 year project, and protect them and the railroad from attacks.

PUFFING BILLY

From England came reports of steam-propelled engines that were replacing horses. An engine called "Puffing Billy," announced in 1813, could haul 10 coal wagons at 5 miles (8 kilometers) an hour. And in 1829, "The Rocket" was invented, the first true Iron Horse. It traveled an amazing 29 miles (47 kilometers) an hour.

A steam-powered engine.

An aerial view of the southern Sierra Nevada Mountains shows the high mountains, deep canyons, and snow that created many challenges for construction crews.

Planners knew it would be a dangerous task to build a railroad to the West Coast. Construction crews would have to cross high mountains, thick forests, burning deserts, and deep canyons. The most dreaded obstacle was the Sierra Nevada, a mountain range that divides California from the rest of the country. The granite mountains rise 4,000 to 7,000 feet (1,200 to 2,135 meters) with 12 peaks higher than 14,000 feet (4,270 meters). The mountain summits were covered with ice much of the year, and snow drifted as deep as 60 feet (18 meters) in winter. Explorers and pioneers had frozen to death trying to cross those mountains.

The debate was interrupted by the Civil War, which divided North and South over the issue of slavery. The war exploded across the country from 1861 to 1865, taking 618,000 lives, ruining the South, and destroying relations between them. Still, in spite of the war, Congress managed to approve a transcontinental railroad, select a route, and build much of it. When the last spike was driven on May 10, 1869, national feelings of pride and triumph helped ease the bitterness and sadness left in the war's wake.

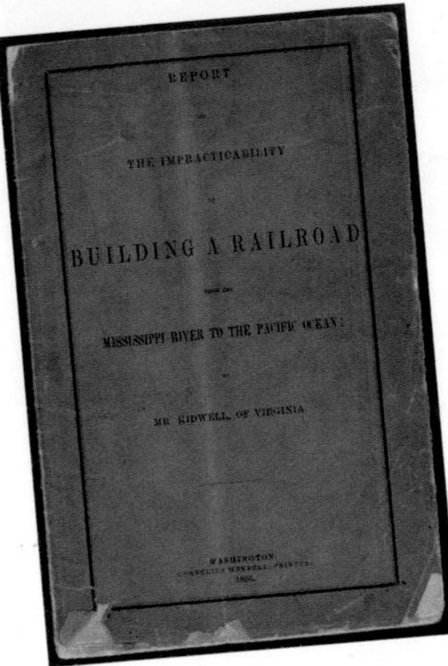
REPORT

THE IMPRACTICABILITY

BUILDING A RAILROAD

MISSISSIPPI RIVER TO THE PACIFIC OCEAN;

MR. KIDWELL, OF VIRGINIA

WASHINGTON:

Government report about the impracticalities of building a railroad.

WESTERN GROWTH BRINGS POWER

During the 1880s, more than 40,000 miles (64,360 kilometers) of railroad track were laid west of the Mississippi River. By 1900 the United States had 14 times as many people as in 1803, and 25 percent of them lived in the West. Historians say that the American people's greatest achievement in the 19th century was ending slavery. But the next greatest achievement was building the transcontinental railroad, which let the country complete its westward growth and emerge as the strongest economic power in the world.

Chapter 2

RAILROAD BRINGS VISIONS OF MONEY AND SPEED

After gold was discovered in California in 1848, building a railroad seemed ever more urgent. It took months of land or sea travel just to get minerals and other goods to market or to bring supplies to miners and settlers. To tap the rich resources of the West, people were convinced everything would have to move much faster.

One of the early supporters of a transcontinental railroad was Asa Whitney, a New England merchant who wanted to trade with China. In 1845, he asked Congress to authorize a survey for a route between the 42nd and 45th parallels. He offered to build the railroad himself if Congress would give him a strip of land 60 miles (96.5 kilometers) wide, reaching from Lake Michigan to the Pacific Ocean. Few at the time took him seriously.

Asa Whitney (1797–1872)

Stephen A. Douglas (1813–1861)

But Americans knew that someday a railroad would be built. And when it happened, whatever route it followed would bring prosperity to that region. Towns and farms would appear along the tracks. Settlers would follow the railroad because they would know that they could recieve supplies and send their farm produce to market.

Cities began competing to become the railroad's eastern **terminus** by holding railroad conventions. Senator Stephen A. Douglas of Illinois wanted the eastern end-point to be Chicago. Southern Senators, such as Thomas Hart Benton of Missouri and Sam Houston of Texas, insisted on a southern route. Major conventions were held in St. Louis, Missouri, Memphis, Tennessee, and other cities, but the only thing people could agree upon was the need for a survey. On March 1, 1853, Congress authorized the Corps of Topographical Engineers to find the most practical and economic route.

The survey's findings, published in 1855, showed that four routes were practical. Senator Douglas proposed that the federal government build three railroad lines. A Northern Pacific line would run from Wisconsin to Puget Sound, Washington, a Central Pacific line would run from Missouri or Iowa to San Francisco, and a Southern Pacific line would run from Texas to Southern California.

It was going to be difficult to pay for even one railroad, and Congress concluded that private **capitalists** would demand rewards for investing so much money. In the past, Congress had given public lands to states, and the states issued bonds to sell to investors, using the money to build railroads. A new way of funding this enormous project was needed. It would involve lending money directly to the railroad companies and giving them large amounts of land on either side of the tracks. The companies could sell the land to help pay for construction.

View from the summit looking west along the 49th Parallel by James Alden, official artist of the U.S. survey team, 1859-1860.

In the midst of this planning, tensions between the North and South were building to intolerable levels. In 1861, 11 southern states **seceded** from the union, triggering the Civil War. With no southern politicians left to argue for a railroad route through the South, Congress selected a central route. Now, someone needed to step forward and build the Central Pacific Railroad.

Theodore Judah, a civil engineer from Connecticut, was that person. He had gone to California to help build a short rail line from Sacramento to the gold fields east of town. He was so eager to build a transcontinental railroad that he could hardly speak of anything else. People who doubted that such a railroad could be built called him "Crazy Judah." After several trips to lobby Congressmen in Washington, D.C., Judah decided to go find the best pass across the Sierra Nevada. In 1860, he explored the mountains and concluded that Donner Summit was the best crossing point.

Theodore Judah (1826–1863)

Judah found four businessmen from Sacramento interested in his ideas. Charles Crocker owned a clothing store, Collis Huntington and Mark Hopkins were partners in a hardware store, and Leland Stanford had a grocery business. These men were active in the new Republican party, and supported Abraham Lincoln, who had just been elected president. Lincoln strongly supported a Pacific railroad. Crocker was a state representative, and Stanford would become California's governor. Their business skills and political connections made them some of the most powerful men in the country. These men were known as the Big Four.

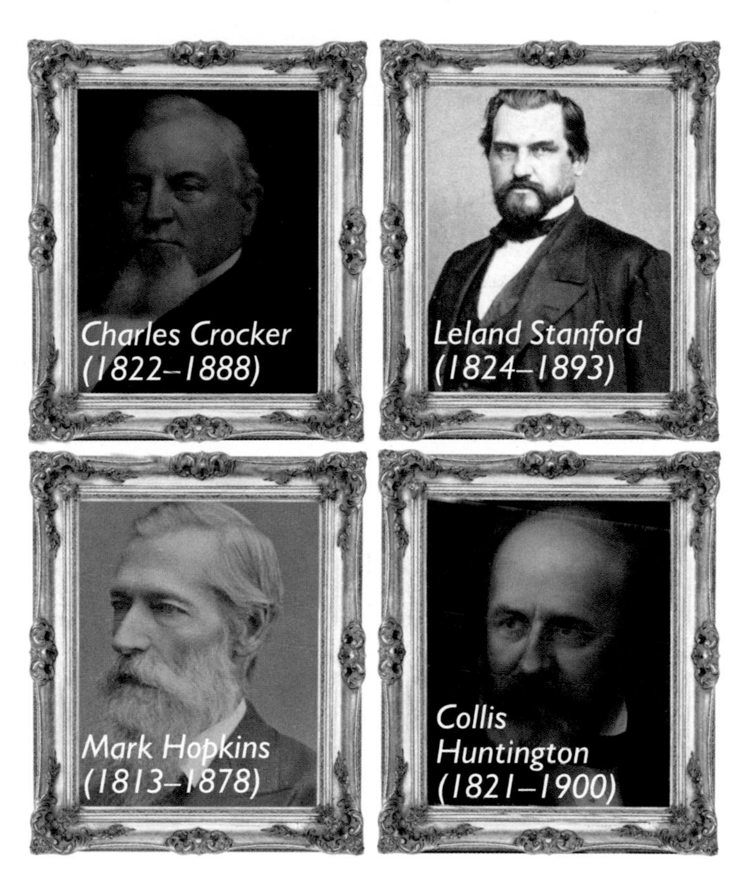
Charles Crocker (1822–1888)
Leland Stanford (1824–1893)
Mark Hopkins (1813–1878)
Collis Huntington (1821–1900)

On June 28, 1861, with the Civil War underway, Judah and his partners incorporated the Central Pacific Railroad of California. Stanford was president and Judah chief engineer. They had a total of $159,000 in assets. But estimates showed it was going to cost $12,500,000 just to cross the Sierra Nevada Mountains!

The Big Four sent Judah to Washington, D.C., to lobby for the railroad. He presented the results of his surveys and offered Central Pacific stock to lawmakers. His hard work paid off when Congress passed and President Lincoln signed a bill authorizing a transcontinental railroad. On July 1, 1862, Judah wired Leland Stanford that his mission had been successful.

DODGE AND LINCOLN

General Grenville Dodge was a Civil War hero who became chief engineer for the Union Pacific in 1866. In 1859, he met Abraham Lincoln, at the time a railroad lawyer running for president. Lincoln's first words to Dodge were, "What's the best route for a Pacific railroad to the West?" Dodge told him to build the railroad in the Platte River valley and later got him to support bills that funded the railroad.

General Grenville Dodge (1831–1916)

Meanwhile, Thomas Durand, a railroad promoter and financier, was promoting his Union Pacific company. He was known for his dishonest dealings, and boasted that his only interest in railroad building was the money to be made.

Union Pacific Railroad logos from 1863 (top) and today (bottom)

Congress chose Union Pacific to build the eastern end of the transcontinental line. The Central Pacific would begin in Sacramento and climb the Sierra Nevada. The Union Pacific would begin at Omaha, Nebraska, cross the Rocky Mountains over South Pass, and meet the California Pacific at the California-Nevada state line.

THE MIDDLE PASSAGE

Today the Interstate 80 highway closely follows the route chosen for the transcontinental railroad. It runs from San Francisco over Donner Pass, through Reno and Elko, Nevada, to Laramie and Cheyenne, Wyoming, and continues from North Platte, Nebraska to Omaha. One difference is that I-80 passes through Salt Lake City, Utah, on the south end of the Great Salt Lake instead of going over Promontory Summit, as the railroad did.

Congress gave each railroad a 400-foot-wide (122-meter-wide) right-of-way for its tracks, yards, and buldings. They also got 10 alternate tracts of land for each mile (1.6 kilometer) of track laid. The land was attractive to the railroad companies because the owners knew land prices would go up along the route. Also, for each mile of track laid in level country, the federal government would loan the company $16,000 at a good interest rate. In the foothills, this amount increased to $32,000 a mile and in the mountains to $48,000 a mile. This deal encouraged railroad companies to lay track in areas more hospitable to settlement.

Union Pacific Railroad Company report, Progress of Their Road.

WHAT THEY RECEIVED

Federal loans to the two companies in the form of 30-year bonds eventually totaled $96 million. The bonds paid six percent interest a year. The Union Pacific received 19.1 million acres (7,735,500 hectares) of land and the Central Pacific about 7.3 million acres (2,956,500 hectares). Both companies made millions of dollars by selling stock and bonds.

The Central Pacific began laying track in 1863, but the Union Pacific took until 1865 to get started. One reason the Central Pacific was more prepared was its close connections with the state of California. The Big Four got the state to lend them $1,659,000 for construction. Also, Stanford and the others loaned the company $60,000 of their own money.

Railroad companies earned $48,000 per mile to lay track through mountain terrain like the Sierra Nevada.

DEATH OF JUDAH

On January 8, 1863, while the first spikes were being driven for the Central Pacific Railroad, Theodore Judah was dying in New York. His relationship with his partners had turned sour, and he had gone east to seek money to buy out the Big Four. Crossing Panama, he caught yellow fever. Judah died on November 2, 1863.

On January 8, 1863, in Sacramento, Charles Crocker supervised the placing of the first rails of the transcontinental railroad. The directors of the Central Pacific held a groundbreaking ceremony. When the locomotive they had ordered was unloaded at the Sacramento dock, it fell into the river. Crocker and Hopkins, who headed the construction crews, hauled it out, named it *Governor Stanford* after their partner, who had been elected California's governor, and sent the locomotive to the newly laid rails.

Typical steam locomotive.

LOCOMOTIVES

The Central Pacific paid $79,752 for two locomotives. The locomotives pulled cars that carried materials, supplies, and men to the construction camps. The cars also provided sleeping and dining quarters. The companies were also able to charge for freight on sections of completed track. In 1865, four years before the transcontinental railroad was completed, the Central Pacific earned $280,000 on freight charges.

Governor Stanford *in the California State Railroad Museum.*

In the East, the Union Pacific held its groundbreaking ceremony on December 1, 1863, in Omaha, but no track was actually built until the middle of 1865. Durant was busy setting up ways in which he could sell shares of his railroad and make money before the first rails were laid. He also distributed shares of the company among politicians to make sure they would vote for bills that favored his activities.

The Central Pacific made slow progress. Only 20 miles (32 kilometers) of rail were laid in 1864, 20 miles (32 kilometers) in 1865, 30 miles (48 kilometers) in 1866, and 46 miles (74 kilometers) in 1867. The war, which ended in 1865, had caused a shortage of materials. Steel rails jumped from $55 a ton in 1861 to $115 in 1863. Railroad building was unbelievably expensive. The 20 miles of track built in 1865 cost $6 million! Realizing that both railroads were struggling for money, Congress passed a new measure giving railroad companies twice as much land, 20 tracts per mile, and more shares were issued. At last, investors began buying railroad stocks and bonds.

HOW RAILROAD OWNERS GOT RICH

Both railroads set up private construction companies. The owners would hire their own companies to lay the track at an inflated cost. For example, the Central Pacific gave its construction arm, the Contract and Finance Company, contracts equal to $90,000,000. But the cost of the work was only $32,200,000. The contracts were paid for by government grants and loans. The Big Four pocketed the difference. The name "Crédit Mobilier," the Union Pacific's construction branch, became a synonym for corruption after its owners transferred federal money to themselves before and during construction.

Chapter 3

THE IMPOSSIBLE ACHIEVED

Charles Crocker supervised construction for Central Pacific. He hired Irish immigrants for the backbreaking work. The men used picks, shovels, carts, and wheelbarrows to remove the dirt and rock. When the grade was even and ties were in place, the rail crews laid steel rails exactly 4 feet 8-1/2 inches (1.44 meters) apart. Then they spiked them in with a sledgehammer, using three blows to each spike. The men earned three dollars a day plus meals.

Chinese workers hammering railroad spikes.

Once they reached the foothills many workers left to work in the Nevada mines. In 1864, 1,900 out of 2,000 men hired left for the mines. So in 1865, Crocker spoke wtih James Strobridge, his construction superintendent, about trying Chinese laborers. More than 25,000 Chinese had come to northern California during the Gold Rush. Strobridge resisted hiring Chinese workers, but Crocker pointed out that the Chinese were willing to for only $25 a month, less than half of what the Irish demanded. They also supplied their own food. "Did they not build the Chinese wall, the biggest piece of masonry in the world?" Crocker asked.

WHERE THE MOUNTAINS STARTED

Stanford's geologists claimed that the base of the Sierra Nevada Mountains started in the Sacramento Valley. Others disagreed, saying the valley was a good 24 miles (38 kilometers) west of where the mountains actually began. Stanford suggested letting President Lincoln decide. But busy with the Civil War, Lincoln simply consented to the geologists' claim. This meant that the Central Pacific could collect a higher price of $48,000 per mile, well before it reached the mountains.

Strobridge agreed to hire 50 Chinese, and if they worked well he would hire more. Within a few weeks Crocker had agents in every California town signing up Chinese men. Strobridge boasted that they were the best workers in the world. By the end of 1865, every available Chinese man in the state was working on the railroad, and Leland Stanford was attempting to bring more from China.

The Central Pacific struggled slowly up the slopes of the Sierra Nevada. In the Sierra, snowdrifts as deep as 60 feet (18.3 meters) were common, settling into ice walls as hard as iron in the spring. Using pickaxes and powder, the Chinese inched their way through these frozen walls. After the harsh winter of 1867, the Central Pacific built wooden snow sheds to keep the snow from covering the tracks.

The Chinese workers were experts at working with rock. They decided to blast through Cape Horn, the steep-walled canyon of the American River's North Fork. The workers had reeds from the San Francisco marshes brought in to the construction site. They wove round, waist-high reed baskets similar to those used in China. Hanging in these baskets alongside the canyon's rock face, they drilled holes, tamped in black powder, set fuses, and hollered for the crews above to pull them away as the powder exploded.

Near the summit of the Sierra Nevada, thousands of Chinese dug and blasted their way through the mountains. Eight thousand men worked in three shifts, night and day, building 12 tunnels from 800 to 1,650 feet (244 to 503 meters) in length at altitudes above 6,000 feet (1,830 meters) in temperatures below freezing.

Back east, after finally beginning construction in June 1865, the Union Pacific had a slow start. By the end of the year, it had laid only 40 miles (64 kilometers) of track from Omaha. But when the Civil War ended, hundreds of Irish laborers came searching for work. By late 1866 the Union Pacific was installing at least one mile (1.6 kilometers) of track a day.

NITROGLYCERIN

Black powder could be used to break granite, but **nitroglycerin** was quicker and more effective. However, it is a highly unstable compound. When a dockhand in Panama dropped a crate of it that was bound for California, he blew himself and dozens of other workers to pieces. A similar explosion blew up the Wells Fargo freight office in San Francisco. But because it sped up the work, Strobridge used it in the Sierra Nevada, especially in the Summit Tunnel. Using nitro, workers were able to build two feet (0.61 meters) of tunnel a day.

Chinese immigrants hand drilled holes into which they packed black powder and later nitroglycerine.

Two examples of trestle construction.

TRESTLE CONSTRUCTION

In 1865 California engineers decided to build wooden trestles to bridge the gaps that the train had to cross. The trestles were supported on the trunks of enormous trees set into masonry. Crews cut giant firs, pines, and redwood trees and shipped them to Sacramento where they were milled into lumber and sent back. The crews built trestles as high as 100 feet (30.5 meters). The tressles resembled giant insects. Though they looked rickety, trestles were strong enough to support a train with many cars.

In early 1866, Durant put two brothers in charge of Union Pacific construction. Dan Casement managed logistics, while John Casement supervised the crews. When Grenville Dodge left the Army and joined the company in May 1866, the construction camps began operating like a military unit. An advance guard went into the countryside to survey the land. They were followed by graders, who cut through gorges, graded the roadbed, and built bridges. Then came the main army to place the ties, lay track, spike down the rails, adjust the alignment, and get the road ready for use. Behind them rolled the construction train cars. One car carried tools, one contained a blacksmith shop, another had dining tables and a kitchen, and other cars held bunk beds. Several **flatcars** carried road-building materials.

Surveying instruments and measuring sticks strongly contributed to making highly efficient railroad systems in the late 1800s.

The Union Pacific crew had rhythm: 4 rails placed a minute, 3 strokes to a spike, 10 spikes to a rail, 400 rails to a mile. Every 30 seconds, the track boss shouted "Down!" signaling the men to drop the rails into place. The Irish crews sang in time, making up songs such as "Whoops Along, Luiza Jane," "Pat Maloy," and "I'm a Rambling Rake of Poverty, the Son of a Gambolier."

The Casement brothers paid each man three dollars a day if the crew laid at least a mile and a half of rail. When they laid two miles (3.2 kilometers) a day, the pay went up to four dollars. But in the summer of 1866, news arrived that made the companies want to move even faster. Congress had decided that the Central Pacific should lay track into Nevada and beyond until the two lines came together. Now, the race began in earnest because all government subsidies, loans, land grants, and fares that were attached to each mile of rail would go to the company responsible for building that mile.

In the summer of 1867, Central Pacific crossed the summit of the Sierras. By the end of that year, Union Pacific had passed Cheyenne, Wyoming. Grenville Dodge, in charge of choosing the route, drove it over the Laramie Hills and across Wyoming to the top of the Rocky Mountains. Thomas Durant telegraphed Stanford in the West: "We send you greeting from the highest summit our line crosses between the Atlantic and the Pacific Oceans, 8,200 feet above tidewater." Stanford replied: "Though you may approach the union of the two roads faster than ourselves you cannot exceed us in earnestness of desire for that great event. We cheerfully yield you the palm of superior elevation; 7,042 feet has been quite sufficient to satisfy our highest ambition. May your descent be easy and rapid."

Westward America *is a mural that depicts the evolution of transportation on the plains, from Indian travois to modern airplanes.*

General William Sherman, who had led Union forces in the Civil War, was responsible for keeping peace with the Sioux, Cheyenne, and other Plains tribes. When Durant gave him a ride on the first 16 miles (25.7 kilometers) of rail, Sherman remarked, "This is a great enterprise but I hardly expect to live to see it completed."

As the railroad crossed the Plains, Native Americans knew it would pose a great threat to their way of life. Unlike emigrants, who passed through their lands, the people brought by the railroad stayed and built towns. This invasion would destroy the buffalo and with it the entire Plains culture. So the Sioux, Cheyenne, Arapaho, and others struck back.

General William Sherman in council with members of the Sioux.

Pawnee in front of a large earth lodge.

The Sioux and Cheyenne attacked construction crews several times during 1867. They pulled up track, derailing a locomotive and killing its engineer and brakeman. Sherman sent four companies of Pawnee, who were enemies of the Sioux and Cheyenne, to guard construction crews. But the Southern Cheyenne wrecked another Union Pacific freight train at Plum Creek, Nebraska, killing the crew. Meanwhile the Sioux had attacked surveyors in Wyoming. Sherman called a meeting with the tribes at Fort Laramie in September 1867. The chiefs tried to explain that the railroad was destroying their way of life, and game was already getting scarce. Sherman replied that they must accept the lands designated for them. "We will build iron roads, and you cannot stop the locomotives any more than you can stop the sun or the moon," he said.

By 1868, the Sioux had been persuaded to sign treaties that moved them to South Dakota, with eastern Wyoming as their hunting ground. The Crow were confined to a section of central Montana, and the other Plains tribes went to reservations in Oklahoma. Although there would still be battles ahead, the nomadic lifestyle of Native Americans had ended.

Chapter 4

JOINING THE TRACKS

In November 1868 Stanford met with Thomas Durant to decide where the railroads would join. Each man stubbornly believed his crew could lay rail faster than the other, and they refused to decide.

As the two companies raced toward each other, they began building less carefully. In their haste, the bosses told themselves that everything could be fixed later. But a few years after the railroad's completion, hundreds of miles of the new railroad had to be replaced. Poorly built rail joints, embankments, and trestles were collapsing. Sharp curves had to be straightened and rough grades reworked. All this work was done at the taxpayers' expense.

Construction of a railroad bridge over the Green River in 1868.

On March 4, 1869, General Ulysses Grant became president of the United States. Four days later, the Union Pacific arrived in Ogden, Utah. Approaching from the West, the Central Pacific was only 50 miles (80.5 kilometers) away, and still no meeting place had been chosen. President Grant ordered Grenville Dodge to bring the parties together and settle the question. Dodge met with Collis Huntington and, after an all-night meeting, came to an agreement. The railroads would join their tracks at Promontory Summit on the north shore of the Great Salt Lake.

As the railroads neared the joining place, the Central Pacific crew proved its skill. Charles Crocker bet Thomas Durant $10,000 that his crew could lay 10 miles (16.1 kilometers) of track in a single day. He selected eight strong Irishmen and Chinese, who put everything they had into the task. Ten Mile Day was April 28. They began at 7:00 a.m. and at 7:00 p.m., James Strobridge declared victory. The eight men, supported by about 1,000 others, had laid 10 miles and 56 feet (16.11 kilometers) of rail. Each of the eight had lifted 250,000 pounds (113,500 kilograms) of iron and spiked 3,520 rails (weighing 560 pounds each) to 25,800 railroad ties. As a bonus, Crocker gave each track layer four days' pay.

On May 8, 1869, Durant was crossing the Sierra by train to witness the railroad joining. The train was stopped by laborers who had not been paid. They refused to let the train continue until Durant paid them $500,000. He wired for money. An assistant wired for troops, but railroad workers intercepted the message. They threatened violence and a strike if troops should arrive. Finally, Durant gave the men $450,000, keeping $50,000, and they released him.

Scene before driving the Last Spike, Promontory Summit, Utah Territory, 1869.

This delay postponed the celebration joining the rails until May 10, 1869. On May 4, David Hewes, a friend of Stanford's, learned that no souvenir had been prepared for the historic event. He quickly had $400 worth of gold made into a 5-5/8 inch (14.4 centimeter) long golden spike. It was engraved with the words "May God continue the unity of our Country as the Railroad unites the two great Oceans of the world." On top of the spike it said "The Last Spike." This spike became famous as the Golden Spike. Three others were made and used in the ceremony. A silver spike from Nevada, a gold and silver spike from Arizona, and a smaller gold spike made by a San Francisco newsman.

Illustration of the Golden Spike.

The Central Pacific's tie contractor had a beautiful railroad tie carved from a California laurel. It was inlaid with a silver plaque that said "The last tie laid on completion of the Pacific Railroad, May, 1869." Because the gold and silver spikes were too soft to hit with a hammer, four holes were pre-drilled into the tie.

Illustration of the last tie.

(Top) A replica of the Central Pacific's Jupiter *and (right) a replica of the Union Pacific's* No. 119.

The two mighty locomotives, *Jupiter* from California, and *No. 119* from the East, stood facing each other about 58 feet (17.6 meters) apart at Promontory Summit. The Union Pacific had built 1,006 miles (1,716 kilometers) of track and the Central Pacific 690 miles (1,110 kilometers). *Jupiter* burned wood and had a round, funnel-shaped smokestack, while *No. 119*, a coal-burner, had a narrow, straight stack. All over the country waiting Americans prepared to celebrate the uniting of East and West.

Workers put the special tie in place and laid the last rail sections across it. Leland Stanford carefully pounded the two golden spikes into the ground. Then Thomas Durant set the Nevada and Arizona spikes. Stanford and Dodge gave short speeches. Workers then replaced the precious metal spikes with iron spikes. Both Stanford and Durant swung at one of the iron spikes with a sledgehammer and missed! The final iron spike was wired to a telegraph line so that the sound of the blow could be heard across the country. A railroad worker hammered the spikes, and Western Union telegraphed the long-awaited message at 12:47 p.m.—D-O-N-E.

Scene after the joining of the tracks at Promontory Summit, Utah, 1869. Jupiter is parked on the left and No. 119 *on the right.*

Church bells rang out across the nation, and even the Liberty Bell in Philadelphia was rung again. Cannons were fired in San Francisco, New York, and Washington, D.C. All across America, people set off fireworks and held parades. Seven thousand people packed the Mormon Tabernacle in Salt Lake City. At Promontory Summit, the locomotives were disconnected and moved forward slowly until they touched. Their engineers blew the whistles, and everyone cheered as workers smashed champagne bottles against the engines. *Jupiter* was backed up and *No. 119* came forward until it sat where *Jupiter* had sat. Then the process was reversed so that each train sat for a moment over the junction of the two lines.

A telegraph pole sticks out above a railroad track. It was used to relay messages across the country.

Stanford held a festive luncheon in his personal railroad car. He and Durant made speeches and sent telegrams to national leaders and other dignitaries. The festivities of the day ended, but the national transformation that it marked had just begun. Within a week, people were riding trains from New York to San Francisco in only seven days! A journey that had once cost $1,000 by wagon now cost from $70 to $150. Mail and freight rates fell drastically as well.

Close-up view of the replica of the Union Pacific's No. 119.

WHERE THE SPIKES AND TIE ARE TODAY

The Golden Spike and silver-plated hammer are in Stanford University Museum in Palo Alto, California. Arizona's spike is at the New York Metropolitan Museum. The laurel tie was in the California Pacific's San Francisco office when it burned to the ground in the earthquake and fire of 1906. On July 30, 1965, the Golden Spike National Historic Site was created near Promontory Summit. Two replicas of the locomotives *Jupiter* and *No. 119* can be seen there, along with replicas of the historic spikes and hammer, and the ceremonial tie. The National Park Service holds reenactments of the Golden Spike Ceremony on May 10 every year.

In 1893, crippled by Durant's mismanagement, the Union Pacific went broke. It was reorganized under new owners and still exists today. The Big Four worked hard to maintain the Central Pacific's **monopoly** in the West. When investors tried to form the Southern Pacific Railroad in 1864, which would connect San Diego with San Francisco and Missouri, the Big Four quickly bought out the line. By the 1880s, the Big Four's transportation network was securely in place.

In spite of the corruption and scandals that accompanied the transcontinental railroad, it transformed America. It linked western mines with eastern markets. The nation's economy was no longer at the mercy of ocean storms, which had sunk many ships, including some carrying gold. Building and running the railroads created a huge demand for timber and coal. Between the 1870s and 1900, railroads consumed more than 20 percent of the nation's timber. Iron and steel production increased ten-fold between 1864 and 1900. Oil had been discovered in Pennsylvania in 1859. Between 1864 and 1900, thanks to railroads, oil production increased twenty-fold.

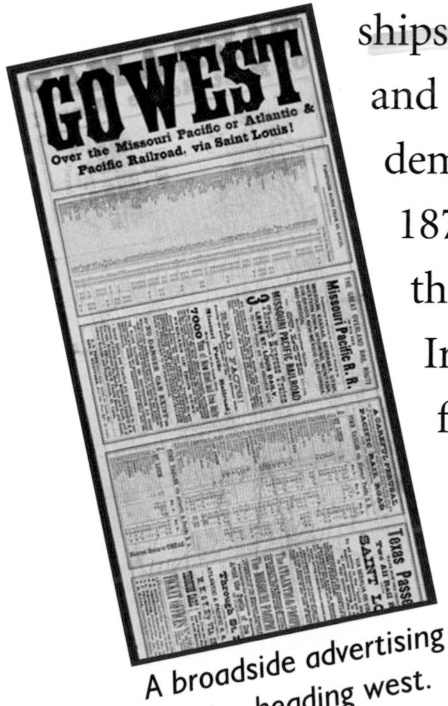

A broadside advertising trains heading west.

Within a few decades, the United States became the world's economic leader. Its internal market was the largest on earth. Crop growers could concentrate on whatever grew best because regions no longer had to be self-sufficient. By 1900, manufacturing output of the United States had passed that of Britain, Germany, and France combined. Although the population had doubled between 1870 and 1900 the United States was able to feed, clothe, and house its citizens better than ever before.

William Henry Jackson, a U.S. geological survey photographer, captured the construction of a railroad bridge in the Green River Valley in the 1870s.

BIOGRAPHIES

Many people played important roles throughout this time period. Learn more about them in the Biographies section.

Jefferson, Thomas (1743–1826) - Third president of the United States (1801-1809).

Stevens, John (1749–1838) - New York inventor and engineer who built the first operating locomotive in the United States.

Allen, Horatio (1802–1899) - American civil engineer and inventor.

Hopkins, Mark (1814–1878) - American merchant and railroad builder.

Durant, Thomas (1820–1885) - A founder of the Union Pacific Railroad; a financier and capitalist.

Sherman, William (1820–1891) - Brigadier general of volunteers during the Civil War; took over command of the Army from General Ulysses Grant in 1869.

Huntington, Collis (1821–1900) - Hardware merchant and railroad builder.

Crocker, Charles (1822–1888) - American merchant and railroad builder.

Hewes, David (1822–1915) - San Francisco contractor and supplier to the Central Pacific Railroad.

Stanford, Leland (1824–1893) - American railroad builder and politician; founder of the Central Pacific Railroad and of Stanford University in Palo Alto, California.

Judah, Theodore(1826–1863) - American civil engineer and railroad surveyor.

James H. Strobridge (1827–1921) - Miner and railroad builder from Vermont, took charge of the Central Pacific's construction in 1864.

Casement, John (1829–1909) - A construction supervisor of the Union Pacific line. Went on to build other railroads across the country.

Dodge, Grenville (1831–1916) - Civil War general and chief engineer of the Union Pacific Railroad construction.

Casement, Dan (1832–1881) - Shared construction supervision responsibility of the Union Pacific line with his brother, Jack.

TIMELINE

1826
First American railroad (horse-drawn) opens in Massachusetts.

1829
Horatio Allen brings an Iron Horse from England and tests it at a Pennsylvania coal mine.

1840
There are 3,000 miles (4,800 kilometers) of railroad lines in the East.

1859
Abraham Lincoln and Grenville Dodge discuss the best route for a Pacific Railroad.

1860
Theodore Judah surveys the Sierra Nevada for a crossing point.

1861-1865
The American Civil War.

1862
Congress passes and President Abraham Lincoln signs the Pacific Railroad Act. It names two companies and directs them to build a transcontinental railroad.

October 1863
The Central Pacific begins construction east from Sacramento, California.

December 1863
The Union Pacific breaks ground at Omaha, Nebraska, but lack of funding delays construction.

1864-1868
The Southern Pacific Railroad is formed and the Central Pacific acquires it to stamp out competition.

1865
The Union Pacific lays its first track from Omaha. The Central Pacific solves its manpower shortage by hiring Chinese construction workers.

1867
The Central Pacific finishes the summit tunnel and crosses the crest of the Sierra Nevada Mountains.

1867-1868
Attacks on the railroad by Sioux, Cheyenne, and other Plains tribes bring about their removal to reservations.

May 10, 1869
A ceremony marks the driving of the final spikes of the transcontinental railroad at Promontory Summit, Utah.

1871-1889
Chartered in 1864, the Northern Pacific Railroad breaks ground and is built between Olympia, Washington, and western Montana.

1965
The Golden Spike National Historic Site is created near Promontory Summit.

REFERENCE

The Transcontinental Railroad Route, 1869

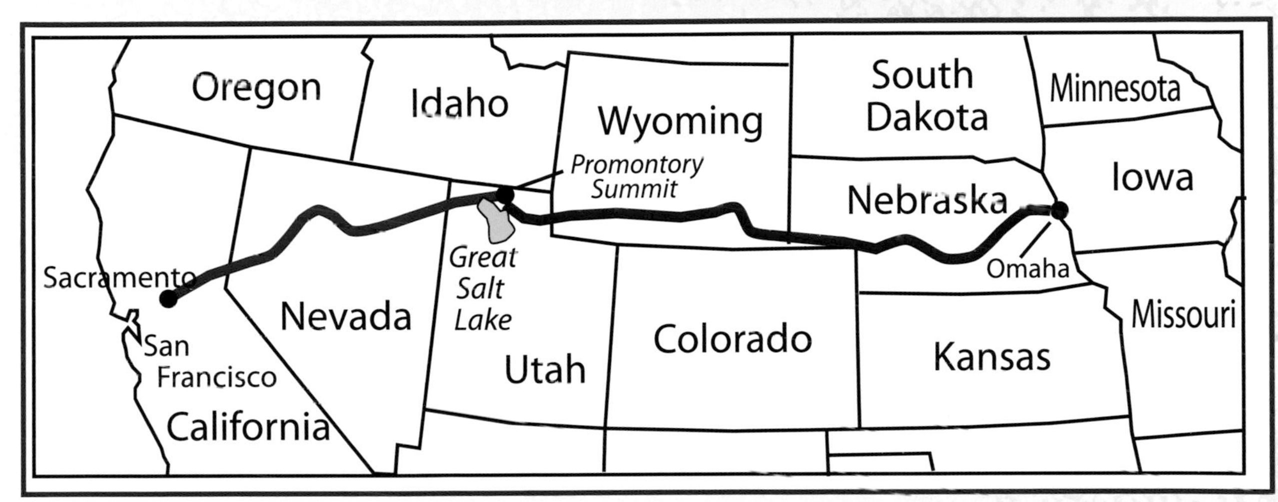

Population Growth Across the Plains, 1870-1900

State	1870	1880	1890	1900
Colorado	39,864	194,327	413,249	539,700
Kansas	364,399	996,096	1,428,108	1,470,495
Montana	20,595	39,159	142,924	243,329
Nebraska	122,841	452,402	1,062,656	1,066,300
North Dakota	2,405	36,909	190,983	319,146
Oklahoma Territory	no data	no data	258,657	790,391
South Dakota	11,776	98,268	348,600	410,570
Texas	818,579	1,591,749	2,235,527	3,048,710
Wyoming	9,118	20,789	62,555	92,531
Total	**1,389,577**	**3,429,699**	**6,143,259**	**7,972,172**

Source: *Historical Statistics of the United States*

WEBSITES TO VISIT

www.freightcapital.com/transportation-history.html

www.tcrr.com

www.history.com/topics/transcontinental-railroad

SHOW WHAT YOU KNOW

1. Describe how people traveled before the transcontinental railroad was built.
2. How was the transcontinental railroad funded?
3. Why was there a need for a transcontinental railroad?
4. How was the joining of the East and West celebrated?
5. How did the railroad change America?

GLOSSARY

capitalist (KAP-uh-tuh-lizt): person who invests money in business; a believer in the economic system that features private ownership of wealth

flatcar (FLAT-kar): railroad freight car with no permanent raised sides, ends, or covering

monopoly (muh-NOP-uh-lee): exclusive ownership, possession, or control

nitroglycerin (NYE-truh-GLISS-ur-in): heavy, oily, explosive liquid used in making dynamite

nomadic (NOH-mad-ik): roaming about from place to place, without a fixed home

secede (si-SEED): to withdraw from an organization or nation

terminus (TURM-muh-nus): final goal; end of the line

transcontinental (transs-kon-tuh-NEN-tuhl): extending across a continent, such as a railway

INDEX